AF344538

UNIVERSITY *of* GUELPH

Happy memories,

[signature]

Dear Brenda,

with kindest regards

Amar

Guelph
March 13, 2012

UNIVERSITY *of* GUELPH

RICHARD BAIN

Foreword by

ROBERTA BONDAR

Published in 2005 by
Binea Press, Inc.
512-1673 Richmond Street
London, Ontario, Canada N6G 2N3
Tel: 519.660.6424
Fax: 519.660.4449

E-mail: bineapress@bellnet.ca
www.bineapress.com

Distributed by:

Binea Press Inc.
519.660.6424

University Bookstore
University of Guelph
519.824.4120 ext. 53715

National Library of Canada Cataloguing in Publication

Bain, Richard (Richard G.), 1954-

University of Guelph / Richard Bain

Photography by Richard Bain; Foreword by Roberta Bondar

ISBN 0-9736863-2-4
1. University of Guelph – Pictorial University Works. I. Title

LE3.G7B34 2005   378.713'43'0   C2005-906239-8

09   08   07   06   05   1   2   3   4   5

Design by Susan Williams
Brian Williams & Associates
London, Ontario, Canada
Tel: 519.657.1529
E-mail: swilliams@on.aibn.com

Printed in Canada by Friesens Corporation
Altona, Manitoba

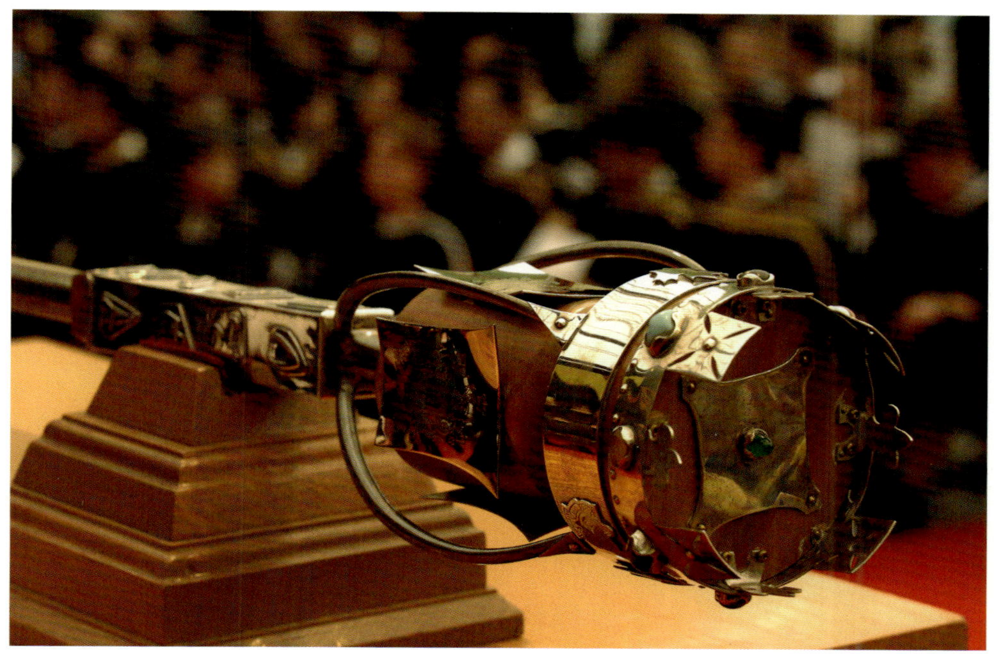

This book is dedicated on behalf of all University of Guelph faculty,

staff, students and alumni to our beloved Chancellor

The Honourable Lincoln M. Alexander

You inspire and encourage us with your deep commitment to the University of Guelph

and your belief in the value and potential of each and every member

of the University community. You personify the heart and soul of this great institution,

and for your leadership, wisdom, warmth and wit, we are forever grateful.

Whether I look at the world through the window of a space shuttle, a microscope or a camera lens, my first reaction is often the same – unbelievable! Whatever the perspective, I cannot help but be amazed by the intricate and unique beauty of life on planet Earth.

Yet, there is always more to know and understand than is captured in one image. This is one of the most important lessons I learned at the University of Guelph. When I look at photographs of the campus tcday, my mind reaches into the memories of friendships and fun and the excitement of discovering someth ng new in a laboratory or a lecture hall.

I clearly recall my residence room in Macdonald Hall, above the front door. It's the safe place that I moved into when I left my family home in Sault Ste. Marie, Ont. Johnston Green still looks much the same, and I trust that today's students are meeting friends there as I did when I came to Guelph in 1964.

My body was well-nourished in Creelman Hall and well-tested during all of the campus sports and social activities that I could cram into a day. My memories also include being quarantined for two weeks to keep from infecting other students with the mumps.

When I think back on U of G, I remember happy times, with faces of friends, times of laughter, time spent studying and learning exciting new things, and time protected to contemplate the direction my life could take me.

Now, when I get together with my classmates, we relive our many Guelph stories and compare notes about the professors who taught our labs and lectures in the Biology Building on Gordon Street. We were the first students to use the Chemistry and Microbiology Building, which was opened in 1965 and demolished this year to make way for a spectacular new science complex. I know that the students who look into microscopes there or through a camera lens in the Zavitz Hall photography studio will be building the same kind of memories.

In my 18 years as a university student (without repeating one year!), the first four years at Guelph were among the most important. For me, they were as revealing as flying in the space shuttle. Both experiences left me with a whole new view of science, my future and my abilities, preparing me for the real world. Since my space flight on *Discovery*, I've been inspired to share a new vision of medicine that includes the health of our planet and our ability to meet emerging challenges.

The University of Guelph is a place where challenges can be faced in a non-threatening environment. Each new generation of students is challenged to reach its academic potential and encouraged to challenge prevailing thought. The University's faculty and staff meet the challenge of adding to our body of knowledge, and its graduates face myriad global challenges.

The vista captured by Richard Bain's lens gives us a sense of the depth of the University of Guelph. These images will rekindle our memories and renew our ability to be amazed.

Roberta Bondar, OC
B.Sc.(Agr.) '68
Scientist, Astronaut, Passionate Earthling

War Memorial Hall was dedicated in 1924 to the memory of Guelph students
and graduates who died in the First World War.

*The University of Guelph is one of the most distinguished
centres of higher education in Canada and the United States,
ranking very high for both research and learning.*

John Kenneth Galbraith, OC
BSA '31
Professor Emeritus, Harvard University

Two stained glass windows in the War Memorial Hall chapel represent war and peace.
One bronze plaque lists the college men who died in the First World War;
the second plaque was added to commemorate those who sacrificed
their lives in the Second World War.

RIGHT: A student enjoys a quiet moment in the lobby of Johnston Hall.
Since opening in 1932, it has served as both a residence and the
administration building for the Ontario Agricultural College.

On Labour Day weekend, more than 1,700 students move into South Residences,
one of the largest university residence buildings in Canada.

*The University of Guelph provides a unique and, from my experience,
ideal environment for personal growth and development. It is small enough
to have a personal touch and big enough to attract first-class educators from around
the world. As a centre for learning, the University enjoys top-tier status in a number
of disciplines and a solid reputation for preparing students to meet the challenges
of today's highly competitive and rapidly changing world environment.
At the same time, the campus retains a beauty and community focus that makes
the Guelph experience so appealing to each new generation of students.*

Warren Jestin
BA '71, MA '71
Board of Governors, Board of Trustees
Senior Vice-President, Scotiabank

First-year students and volunteers enjoy the "festival" atmosphere of Orientation week.

New Guelph students enjoy a lesson in African drumming,
an Aboriginal dance performance, a pep rally and getting to know the campus.

Guelph students head home for spring break.

*Our Aboriginal students come from diverse backgrounds
across North America. Maintaining and enhancing our identities
by sharing traditions, languages and stories are integral parts of
the campus experience. The University of Guelph is a great environment
to express our identities with each other and among
our non-Aboriginal brothers and sisters.*

Jaime Mishibinijima
Aboriginal Student Adviser

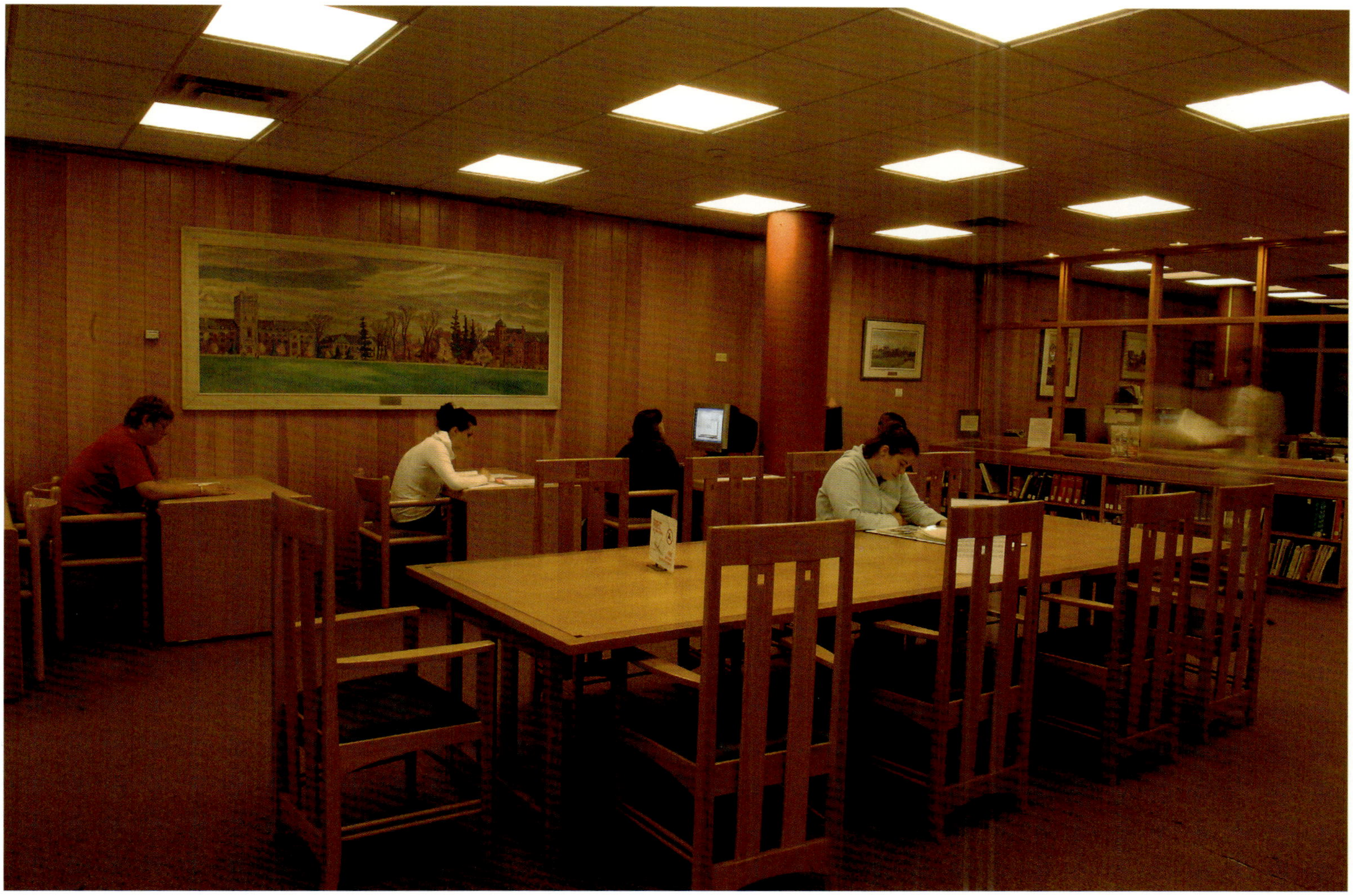

Top: The University Library welcomes visitors from around the world to its Archival and Special Collections.

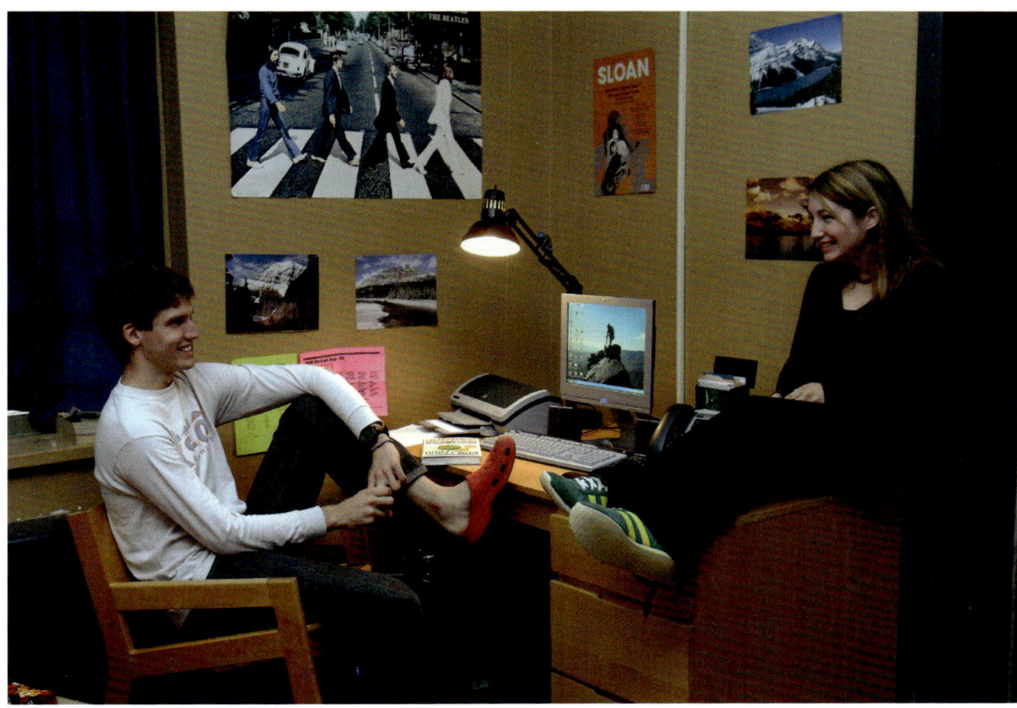

Friends hang out in Mills Hall.

Students who choose the Creelman Hall dining room and adjacent food court know why Guelph is a recognized leader in university food service.

*The University of Guelph is unique for its dedication
to quality of life and for its unwavering commitment
to the people who make up its community.
I came to Guelph with ideas and enthusiasm, left with strong
values and close friendships. The physical campus has
changed and grown, responding to the expectations
of government, business and society,
but the rural-inspired spirit of the
three founding colleges will thrive indefinitely.*

William T. Brock
BSA '58, Hon. Fellow '98, H.D.La. '02
Board of Governors, Board of Trustees

Speeding across campus on a summer day.

Top: Lingering after class outside the MacLachlan Building.

Bottom: Resting with Old Jeremiah.

Spring arrives at the University of Guelph.

Aiden Abram
Undergraduate Student, International Development
and Earth Surface Science
Co-chair, U of G United Way Campaign

Exam time means a mental workout in the Mitchell Athletics Centre main gym.

Students mingle with faculty and staff in the University Centre dining area.

The 'Ring
Coffee Pub

War Memorial Hall is used for ceremonies, cultural events and class lectures.

*It is because of our students that the University of Guelph has
a reputation as a campus that cares. Our students support other students
in all corners of the University and reach into the community
as volunteers for many of Guelph's service agencies.
A university is a place to learn and grow. At Guelph,
much of the learning occurs outside the classroom
in programs initiated by and for students.*

Brenda Whiteside
BA '82 and MA '83
Associate Vice-President (Student Affairs)

Snow covers Reynolds Walk in front of the Crop Science Building.

Winter weather doesn't
stop the action on campus.

Guelph students have access to library resources totalling 7.5 million items thanks to a unique partnership with neighbouring university libraries.

Late winter brings more snow, sunshine and outdoor fun.

*The University of Guelph is one
of Canada's most beautiful campuses,
and we want to maintain a grand
vision through our campus master plan
that pays tribute to the historical
architecture and green spaces that
define this institution.*

Douglas Derry
Chair, Board of Governors
Chair, Poplar Lane Holdings Ltd.

Guelph alumni raised the funds
needed to refurbish and maintain
the Rutherford Conservatory
Greenhouse and Gardens.

The portico on Johnston Green is one of the most popular sites
in Guelph for wedding photography.

Open every day from dawn to dusk, the Arboretum welcomes more than 73,000 visitors each year.

Spring in the Arboretum and on the main campus.

Left: Wild Goose Swamp in the Arboretum.

Below: A flowering crab tree and water lilies.

The fine art studios in Zavitz Hall overlook Branion Plaza.

TOP RIGHT: The Macdonald Stewart Art Centre is the repository for the University of Guelph art collection.

RIGHT: Prof. John Kissick, director of the School of Fine Art and Music, takes time to enjoy the school's extensive print collection.

Works of art in the Donald Forster Sculpture Park
and the MacKinnon Building.

The main building of the Ontario Veterinary College.

ONTARIO VETERINARY
COLLEGE
Ontario Veterinary
Main Building

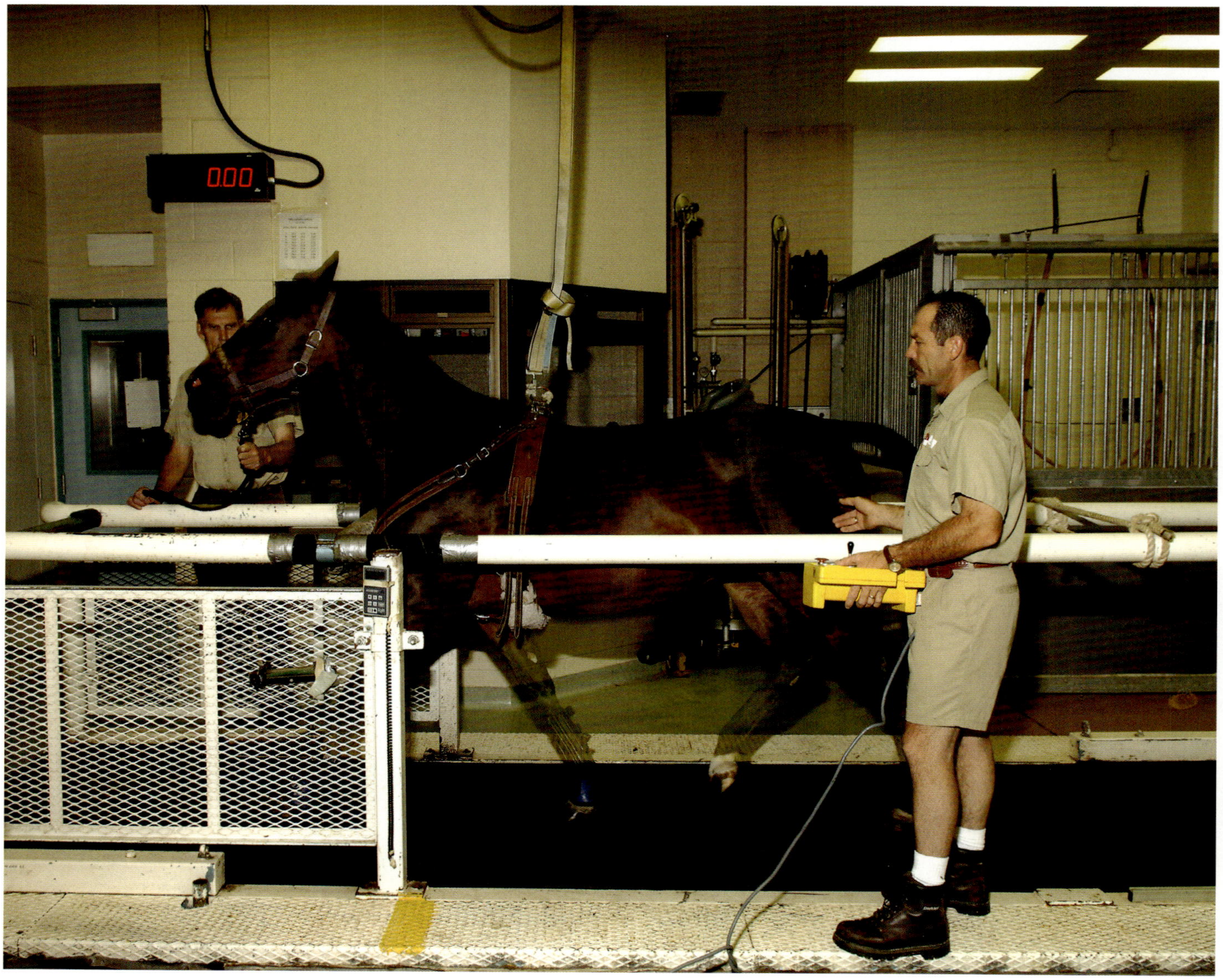

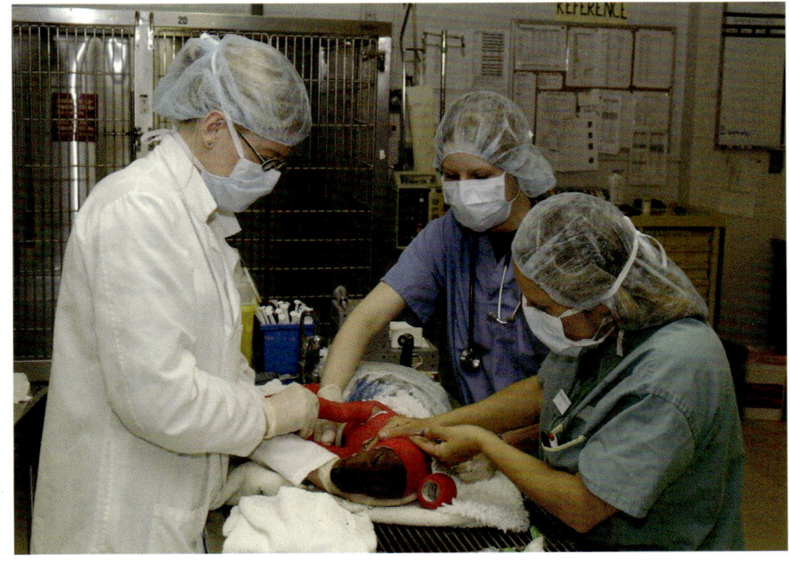

Guelph's veterinary college
is world-renowned for its research,
teaching and clinical-care programs.

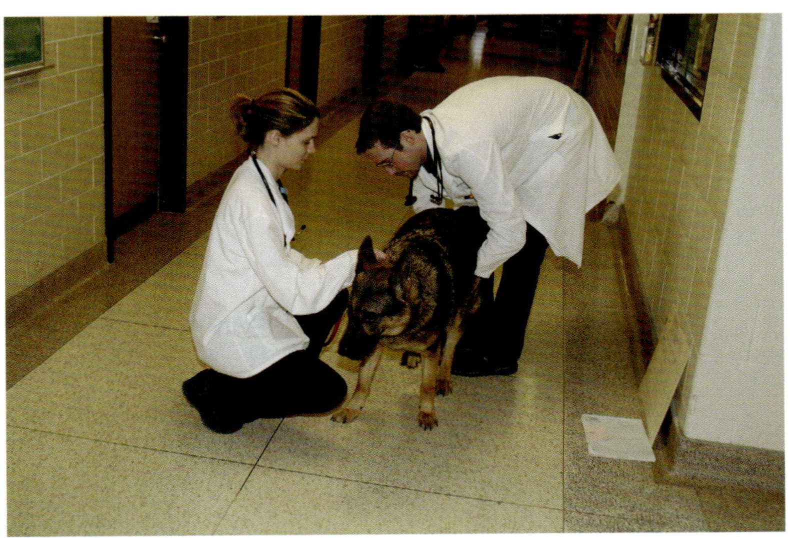

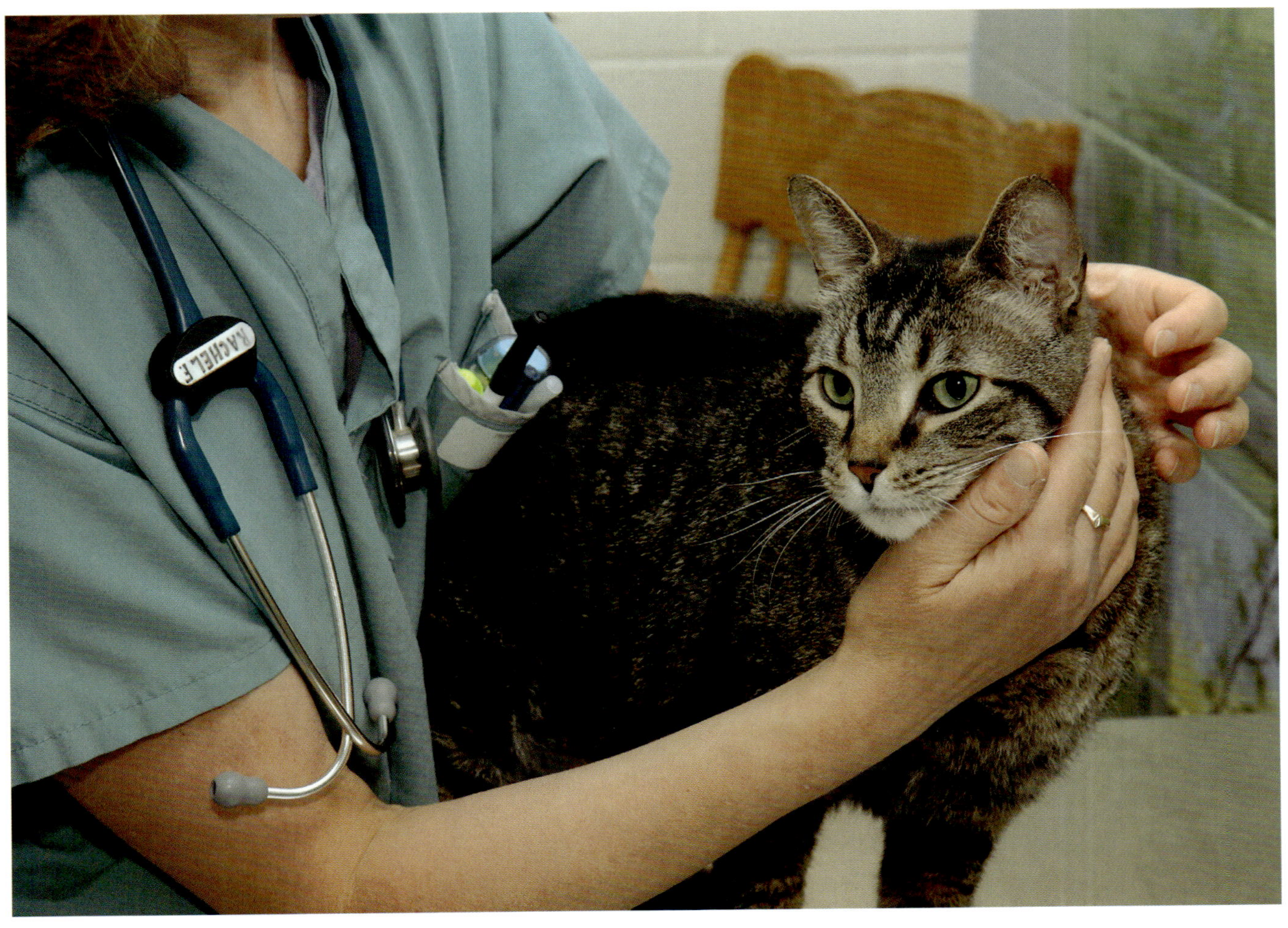

The Hutt Building is home to the University's Department of Geography.

Tending plant specimens in the Department of Crop Science greenhouse.

Academic counsellor Evie Adomait teaches an introductory economics course in Rozanski Hall. The multimedia classroom complex can accommodate 1,530 students in lecture halls ranging in size from 30 to 600 seats.

Students help each other in a 70-seat computer lab located in the School of Engineering's Thornbrough Building.

In the University of Guelph's new science complex, Prof. Joseph Lam, Molecular and Cellular Biology, works with PhD candidate Wayne Miller and research assistant Erin Anderson (in background) to purify a protein that will be used as a drug target. On the opposite lab bench, graduate student Kasia Kaluzny reads a protocol. Research in the Lam laboratory is aimed at helping cystic fibrosis sufferers lead longer and healthier lives.

Prof. Frances Sharom and post-doctoral researcher Ronghua Liu, Molecular and Cellular Biology, use a fluorescent technique to conduct an experiment on a drug efflux protein that is important in cancer treatment.

The Department of Food Science offers the only accredited food science program in Ontario.

Prof. Rickey Yada, bottom photo, leads a new Canada-wide Advanced Foods and Materials Network that researches novel ideas in food safety, nutritional quality and human health.

When Guelph engineering students entered the first four-wheel-drive car in the Society
of Automotive Engineers annual race, they finished 17th out of 140 teams.

Physics professor Robert Brooks and graduate student Christian Schroeder try out their department's new telescope in the MacNaughton Building observatory.

Launched in 2002, the University of Guelph-Humber was the first institution in Canada to offer an integrated university honours degree and college diploma in a four-year program.

Almost 2,000 Guelph-Humber students study in a $45-million facility located on the Humber College campus in Toronto.

The University of Guelph Kemptville Campus has 75 years of history in practical education and research that benefits the agri-food industry.

Aerial photography
demonstrates crop
development at the
University's Ridgetown
Campus, which has
focused on educating
students, research in
crop production and
rural development for
over 80 years.

The Vineland campus along the Niagara Peninsula is home
to over 90 hectares of experimental tender fruits.

Collège d'Alfred, near Ottawa, is part of a province-wide program in waste-water management.

The *Canadiana/Begging Bear* by sculptor Carl Skelton is permanently installed at the bus stop in front of the Macdonald Stewart Art Centre on Gordon Street.

In my memories, it is always a bright autumn day on campus:
yellow leaves, the smell of new paper, and the sense of a fruitful harvest in the nearby countryside.
I left the University of Guelph with a solid body of knowledge, the possession of which would help me observe
and understand the world with greater clarity, and an increased love for the pioneer towns and farms and villages
that were so much a part of the landscape surrounding both the town and the campus.
But most of all, it was during this period of my life that I developed an enthusiasm for enthusiasm itself.
By the time I graduated, I knew for certain that I would need to devote my life, and in particular my writing life,
to the exploration of images and ideas that moved me on an emotional as well as an intellectual level.

Jane Urquhart, OC   BA '71, H.D.Lett. '99
Governor General's Award for Fiction

The East Village townhouse complex provides accommodation for 645 students and includes several townhouses that are completely accessible for people in wheelchairs.

The important relationship between the University of Guelph and its alumni was reaffirmed in 1987 with the opening of Alumni House. The remodelled 1879 barn is the oldest building on campus.

Ontario

The Research Park Centre is central to the University's 12-hectare Research Park, which provides facilities and offices for agribusiness, animal health and molecular design companies while helping them tap into Guelph's research strengths.

LEFT: Through a unique partnership with the Ontario Ministry of Agriculture, Food and Rural Affairs, the University of Guelph also delivers government-sponsored research, education and laboratory services for the agri-food sector.

Macdonald Hall presides over the north campus residences. More than 5,000 single and married students live on campus.

The Bovey Building and its greenhouses are used by the Department of Environmental Biology.

Opened in 2003, Rozanski Hall is a high-tech classroom complex that can accommodate 1,530 students in lecture halls ranging in size from 30 to 600 seats.

Gryphon football has 125 years of history on campus, a national championship victory in 1984
and a reputation for producing exceptional athletes and coaches who have gone on to both
academic and professional sport arenas across North America.

The Gryphon mascot pictured below with Prof. Fred Ramprashad of the College of Biological Science predates the 1970 opening of Alumni Stadium, which was funded primarily by Guelph graduates and Gryphon fans.

Students in the School of Hospitality and Tourism Management
learn to manage a restaurant by taking their turn on the chef's crew.

*The University of Guelph is more than just a place to earn a degree.
Within campus boundaries, students have access to support services
and resources that go well beyond academic issues.
In addition, the campus offers numerous opportunities for students
to get involved in volunteer activities, fostering education in the
broader sense. These are things that I appreciate
very much as a student.*

Amrita Roy
Undergraduate Student, Biomedical Sciences and French
Lincoln Alexander Chancellor's Scholar

The MacKinnon Building provides space for the College of Arts
and the College of Social and Applied Human Sciences.

Gryphon rowers practise on Guelph Lake, the women's basketball team plays at home, and swimmers count lengths in the University's Olympic-size pool.

My years at the University of Guelph
were some of the best of my life.
I loved the campus, and it was beautiful at any time of the year.
I enjoyed the fact that it was convenient to get around;
getting from class to the rink took no time at all.

Cassie Campbell
BA '97
Olympic Gold Medallist, Women's Hockey

Summertime at the Bullring patio and the Science at Guelph Experience (S@GE) camp for kids.

College Royal favourites –
square dancing and the
chemistry magic show.

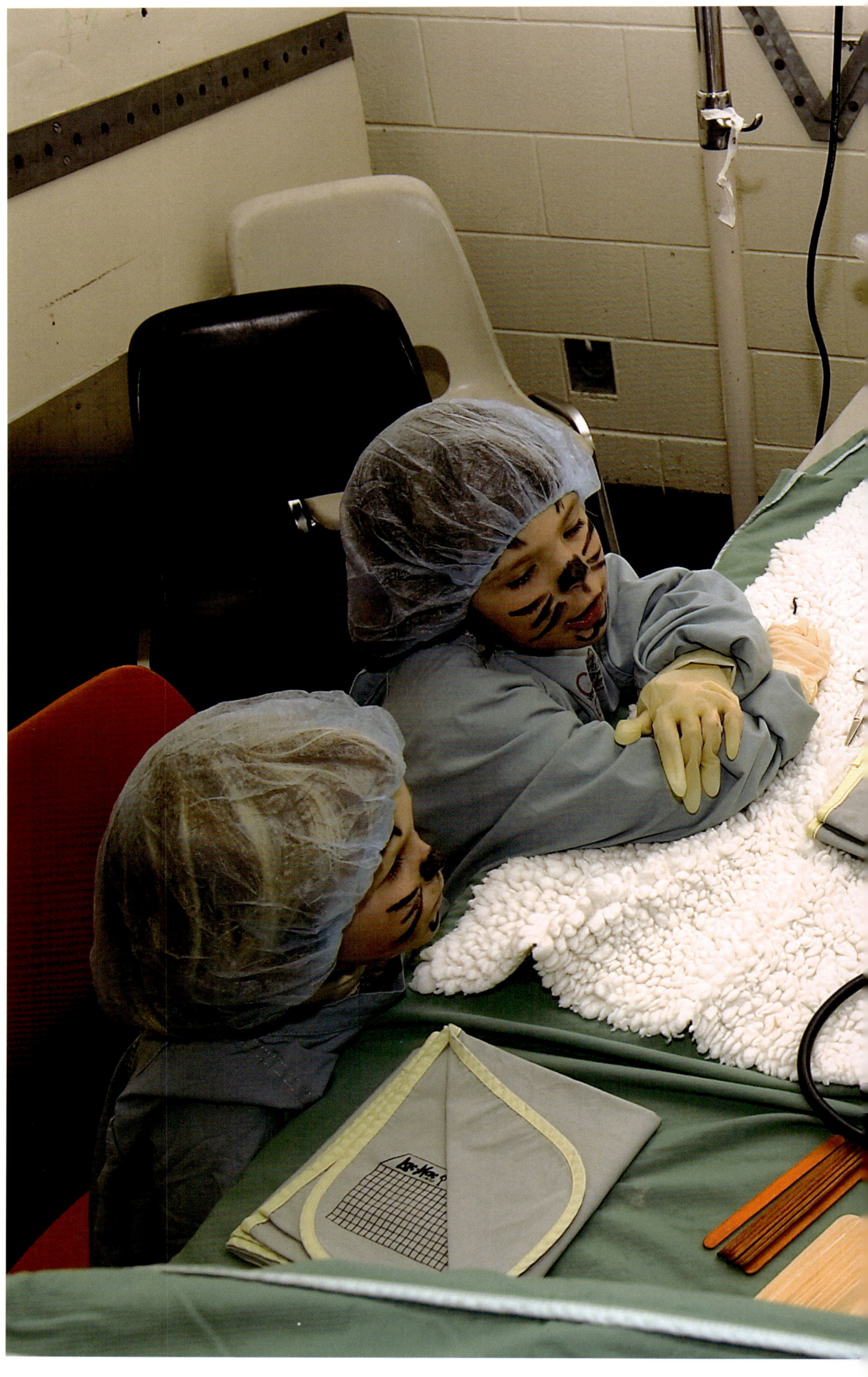

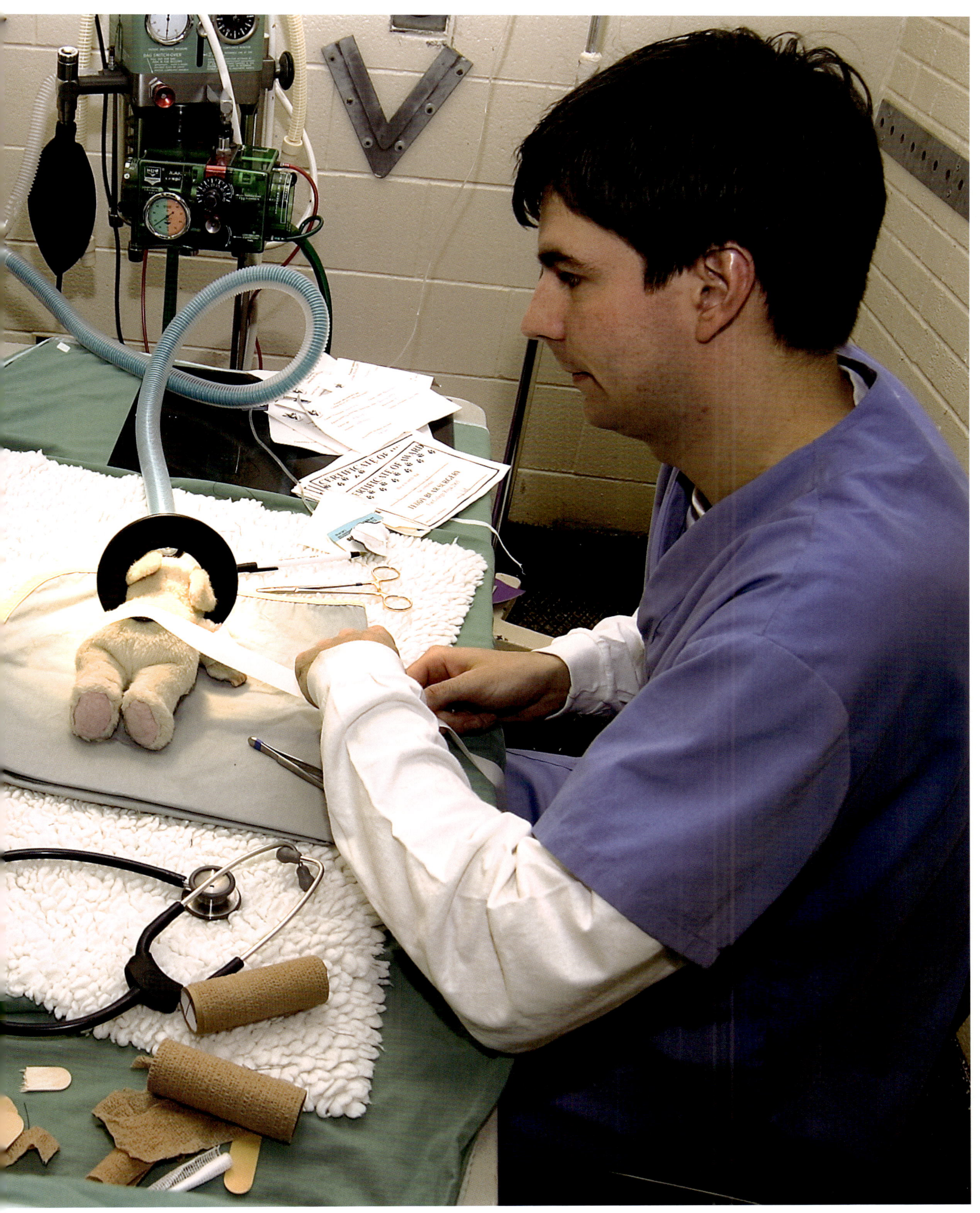

A veterinary student performs teddy bear surgery at College Royal.

College Royal is the largest student-run open house at any university in Canada.

Each year I have the pleasure of
meeting and welcoming thousands
of visitors to the University of
Guelph campus. Together with my
team of tour guides and student
ambassadors, I give prospective
students and their families their first
look at our vibrant, friendly and
beautiful campus. My job truly
makes me feel that I am part of this
amazing community.

Marisa Phillips
Campus Tour Co-ordinator

Summer flowers in a perennial garden frame the University Centre administration building.

University of Guelph president Alastair Summerlee entertains Guelph graduates in the sunroom of the President's House. The stone cottage was built in 1882.

Alumni Weekend at the University of Guelph.

*Our students say they come to the University of Guelph because of the warmth
of the school and the beauty of the campus. We have an appealing balance
of architectural styles that truly reflect the University's history.
The grounds, with an abundance of flowers, green spaces and the Arboretum,
are esthetically awesome. That's not surprising given Guelph's world-class stature in fields
such as horticulture and landscape design. Our campus atmosphere is part of the reason
we attract leading academics and students from around the world, helping us to remain
one of the foremost comprehensive universities in the country.*

The Honourable Lincoln M. Alexander, OC
Chancellor, University of Guelph
Former Lieutenant-Governor of Ontario

As chancellor of the
University of Guelph,
the Honourable
Lincoln M. Alexander
has a special greeting
for each graduate.

Spring Convocation at the University of Guelph is held in the University's new Gryphon Dome.

Convocation celebrates
academic achievement
and the importance
of family and friends.

Looking north on Winegard Walk between the McLaughlin Library, left, and the MacKinnon Building.

MacKinnon
Building

Johnston Green embodies the meaning of the Latin word *campus*, which translates to "field." In this case, it's a manicured pasture filled with stately maple trees, towering spruce and vibrant sumac. Surrounded by historical limestone and red-brick buildings, Johnston Green is the essence of an academic environment.

Enjoying the spring sunshine.

Macdonald Hall opened as a residence in 1904, one year after Macdonald Institute accepted its first female students.

*When I recall Macdonald Institute, my memories
are of an inspiring time and place where aspirations
and ideals were nurtured, shaped and refined.
My classmates and I were blessed with
positive female role models pursuing research and
academia, who bred confidence in those of us who
desired to make a difference in the world, to be
accepted as an equal in any environment and
to be recognized for our contributions.
Today, we are driving meaningful and lasting
change in our communities, business, politics,
education, science and medicine and at home.*

Martha Billes, OC
B.H.Sc. '63
Director, Canadian Tire Corporation
Chair, Canadian Tire Foundation for Families

Daffodils and solitude in the Arboretum.

Native grasses catch the morning sun.

Locust trees frame
Alumni Walk as
the sun sets on
Johnston Green.

ACKNOWLEDGEMENTS

It was a great experience to return to university once again, this time at a different school
but a place that won my heart very quickly. The University of Guelph must be one
of the most academically diverse institutions in Canada, which made this photography project
both a rewarding challenge and a learning experience. Through the University's diversity,
a common thread exists, and that is the sprit and friendliness of the students,
staff and faculty. I was a newcomer to the campus, but everyone I asked for assistance
was only too glad to offer his or her help. They certainly made my job much easier.

It was an honour to have Roberta Bondar – truly an accomplished "passionate earthling,"
agree to share her memories of time spent at Guelph as a student. Working with her
and listening to her talk about her similar passion for photography, which grew, in part,
out of her experience on the space shuttle Discovery, was fascinating. She is a great
ambassador for our country and this university.

Invaluable to the project was the guidance I received from Chuck Cunningham
and Mary Dickieson in the University's Communications and Public Affairs office.
Many others on campus too numerous to mention facilitated my photography,
and I am grateful for your generous help.

A group of distinguished individuals contributed reflective quotes for this book.
Thanks to each of you for sharing your vision and memories of the University of Guelph.

It always seems a small miracle to me how a designer can work with a group of
photographic images to produce a finished work. Thank you to Susan Williams
from Brian Williams & Associates for another excellent publication. Thanks also
to Tom Klassen from Friesens Book Division for co-ordinating the production.

I extend heartfelt thanks to my wife, Joan, who continually encourages me to do what
I am passionate about. Thanks also to our children, Daniel, Caroline, Jordan and Brett,
who always ask how my projects are going. As you each go in different directions,
following your careers or educational paths, may you have the good fortune
that I have had to see so much beauty, and not only through the lens of a camera.

I hope this book keeps the memory alive for those of you fortunate enough to have
an affiliation with this great university. I am envious of those who have had the
opportunity to spend more than the 10 months I did around this campus.
The University of Guelph is a place that truly grows on you, a campus filled
with people and places that touch your heart.

Richard Bain